Meghan on Stage!

★

written by
Lori Z. Scott

illustrated by
Stacy Curtis

Standard PUBLISHING

Cincinnati, Ohio

Published by Standard Publishing, Cincinnati, Ohio
www.standardpub.com

Text Copyright © 2007 by Lori Z. Scott
Illustrations Copyright © 2007 by Stacy Curtis

Printed in: USA
Project editor: Laura Derico
Cover and interior design: Holli Conger

Library of Congress Cataloging-in-Publication Data

Scott, Lori Z., 1965-
    Meghan Rose on stage! / written by Lori Z. Scott; illustrated
by Stacy Curtis.
        p. cm.
    Summary: When her act for the talent show is mistakenly
sabotaged, first-grader Meghan Rose discovers what her
God-given talent is through prayer and proceeds to use it and
bloom. Includes discussion questions and activities.
    ISBN 978-0-7847-2103-2 (perfect bound)
[1. Talent shows—Fiction. 2. Schools—Fiction.
3. Friendship-Fiction. 4. Christian life—Fiction.
5. Humorous stories.] I. Curtis, Stacy, ill. II. Title.

PZ7.S42675Me 2007
[Fic]--dc22
                                                    2007010719

17 16 15 14 13 12   4 5 6 7 8 9 10 11 12

Contents

Meghan Rose

Hi. I'm Meghan Rose Thompson, but you can just call me Meghan. My mom sometimes uses all my names, but that's not usually a good thing. Because then her voice gets louder. And her face turns red. So just Meghan is fine.

My favorite color is blue because I have blue eyes. Also, I have long, straight, brown hair. Brown like bread crusts, mud, and banana bruises. I'd rather have blue hair since brown ranks low on my favorite color list. But I will live.

I go to first grade. My teacher is Mrs. Arnold. She's smarter than even my grandma, I think. She knows a lot about lunch money and staplers and stuff like that.

She always gives us way too much homework, but I think the principal makes her do that, because I don't think she really enjoys grading all those papers.

But guess what? This afternoon Mrs. Arnold told us she wasn't giving us any homework all week. She was too busy organizing the school talent show to mess with it.

We clapped and clapped at that. I tell you, that woman is full of surprises.

Then Lynette Becker raised her hand.

She sits in front of me. Sometimes I can't see over the big frilly hair bows she wears.

Lynette keeps her desk so clean that she never has trouble finding her scissors or crayons. In fact, she seems like the type of person whose favorite color just might be brown.

"Can I be in the talent show? I can play 'Yankee Doodle Dandy' on the piano. I'm sure I will be a star."

Mrs. Arnold held up a finger.

For some reason that always gets Lynette to stop talking. I've never seen anyone control talking with one finger before. But it works for Mrs. Arnold.

"Anyone interested in participating in the talent show can try out next week after school. Just fill out a form with your name and a description of your act, and get your parents to sign their permission. Each grade has its own day to try out. Practice first, and then show up on the right day. After tryouts, I'll notify everyone who makes it into the show."

Lynette started jumping up and down. Mrs. Arnold frowned at her and said, "Trying out doesn't guarantee you'll be selected to perform in the talent show."

"Oh, I know I'll make it, Mrs. Arnold," Lynette said. "Mom says I'm the best piano player in first grade."

Then she started wiggling her fingers in the air and humming "Yankee Doodle."

"Only that's not so great," I interrupted, "because not everyone can play the piano."

Mrs. Arnold smiled. "You don't have to play piano. You can sing or dance or read a poem. Be creative."

Ryan raised his hand. "I could dribble a basketball," he said.

I smiled at that. Ryan is a good friend, and he can dribble something fierce. Plus when he dribbles, his curly hair bounces like a Slinky toy. Which is kind of cool.

"Well, OK," Mrs. Arnold said.

Ryan kept talking. "Or I could burp the alphabet."

Ryan burps really well. I don't know how he does it either. It is a special skill, I think.

Everyone started talking.

"I can dance."

"I'll play my recorder."

"I'll do a cheer!"

With so much blabbering, I had to stand up just to be heard. "AND I'LL SHOW MY BOTTLE CAP COLLECTION."

Everyone went quiet.

And looked at me.

Lynette narrowed her eyes. "You can't do that, Meghan. It's not show-and-tell. You have to go on stage and entertain everyone."

I lifted my chin. "Bottle caps *are* entertaining."

Ryan snorted. "Bottle caps are only entertaining if you are juggling them or using your teeth to bend them into interesting shapes."

"Oh," I said in a small voice.

Ryan gave me the thumbs-up. "But otherwise, you go, girl."

Mrs. Arnold sighed. "Who wants a form?"

Lynette raised her hand and gave me a grinny smile over her shoulder. That bugged me. I could just see her all dressed up in a puffy dress with big hair, body glitter, lip gloss, and tip-tap shoes. And everyone would cheer for her.

I felt a little jealous of that girl. I couldn't play piano. In fact, I couldn't even dribble or burp very well. I didn't know what I'd do, but I gulped and raised my hand too.

I, Meghan Rose, must have *some* kind of talent. Right?

Bubble Gum

Ryan came over to my house after school. He pulled out a pack of green bubble gum, the kind that tastes like sour apples. We sat on the back porch, all quiet and thinking. Except he also chewed. And popped his gum. Again. And again.

I frowned. "Stop blowing bubbles. I need to think."

Pop. Pop. "Why?"

I stamped my foot. "Because unlike you,

I can't dribble or burp or blow bubbles very well. I can't play piano either, which isn't even half as interesting. So I will have to think of something else to do for this talent show."

Ryan shrugged. "I can blow bubbles and dribble at the same time."

"That doesn't help me," I growled.

"Got a basketball?"

I pointed. "Under the bush."

He scooped up the basketball. *Dribble. Pop. Dribble.*

I admit, the boy was good. *Dribble. Pop. Dribble.*

The beat made an idea pop *BLAM* into my head. "I know what to do. I'll sing!"

Ryan stopped dribbling. "Please don't sing. Last time you sang, I thought a bee had stung you or something."

"Don't be ridiculous. I am so honeybee sweet, bees love me."

"Oh, right."

"I will sing 'God Bless America.'" I slapped my hand over my heart.

"God bless America.

Land that's a club!

Stand beside her.

And hide her.

Through the fights and the bites

    from above.

From the fountains.

Toothy fairies.

Do the motion—"

Then I stopped. "What comes after that?"

Wincing, Ryan took his fingers out of his

ears. "Nothing. Honest."

"Maybe I should try a different song."

Ryan held out his pack of bubble gum. "Maybe you should try a piece of gum. We could blow bubbles together. Like those synchronized swimmers in the Olympics. That takes talent."

"Yeah, only I can't blow bubbles."

Ryan's mouth fell wide open. "You can't blow bubbles at all?"

I shrugged. "Nope."

"Tell you what," Ryan said. "You try blowing a bubble, and I'll figure out what you're doing wrong."

He handed me some gum. I chewed and chewed that sour stuff and didn't even make a face. I also made some great smacking noises.

Ryan watched. "Your chewing looks

good. Now use your tongue to make a flat wall of gum, and then push your tongue into the middle of it."

I made a flat wall of gum. Then I pushed my tongue into it.

"Hoo dooth it look?" I said. It's hard to talk with your tongue sticking out.

Ryan nodded. "That looks good too."

"Thood I bwoow now?"

"Pull your tongue back in first, and then blow."

I did. Nothing happened. "See, I can't do it."

"You didn't blow hard enough. Try again."

So I chewed and pushed and blew again. This time I made a little bubble, but it popped right away.

"Wowie!" I said. "There's hope!"

Ryan moved closer. "Try it again, but blow harder."

I chewed really hard. I pushed out my tongue really hard. Ryan leaned forward. "Now BLOW!"

I took a big breath. And I blew. Really hard.

FFWOOOOOOMMMM!

The gum flew right out of my mouth. I tell you, it looked like a gooey, green rocket. And SPLAT! That gum hit Ryan smack on his forehead.

Ryan's face turned red. His eyes bulged like a frog's eyes. And he started jumping up and down, also like a frog, yelling, "Oh, GROSS, GROSS, GROSS, GROSS!"

He tried pulling the gum off, but it got stuck in his hair.

"Oops," I said. "Sorry." Then I gave him

a thumbs-up. "But good news! Now we know what is wrong in my bubble process. I am blowing challenged."

"Yeah. Well, you blew it. Lesson over. You can't be in my act."

I bit my lip. "Oh."

"How am I going to get the gum out of my hair?"

"I have scissors in the kitchen. Do you want me to cut it out?"

Ryan sighed. "OK. Only don't cut off all my hair."

Feeling the sticky spot with his fingers, Ryan moved toward the house. "Could you bring in my backpack for me? I am too crazed by grossness to carry it in."

I didn't want to let my friend down after I'd gummed him up. That would be impolite, I think. With a grunt, I lifted his backpack.

That thing was loaded.

"What's in here?" I gasped.

"My entire comic book collection. Need help?"

"Don't worry. I got it. It's as light as a rock," I wheezed, dragging that pack along.

I told you I was honeybee sweet.

Kangaroo Bouncy

At recess the next day, I sat on a bench and watched Ryan play basketball. He now had a short, short, short, short, short haircut. You see, cutting gum out of hair is not as easy as it looks. I had to keep evening it out.

Apparently I am not destined to be a hair stylist when I grow up. Or a piano player. Or a bubble gum blower. But I will live.

Kayla plopped down next to me.

Kayla is also in my class, and she is extra

bouncy. Like kangaroo bouncy. Which is why we like jumping rope together. Because, let me tell you, I am kangaroo bouncy too.

Kayla is short with piggy-tailed, blond hair. That is a fun combination, I think. Also, she is missing a tooth. I do not hold that against her.

Kayla wiggled the jump rope in front of me. "Come on, Meghan! Let's jump."

I slouched. "I do not feel like jumping rope today. I have figure-out-what-to-do on my mind."

Kayla made a face. "What are you figuring out?"

"I am trying out for the talent show," I said, "but I need an act."

"Oh," Kayla said. She patted my leg and slouched with me. That is one of the things I like about Kayla. She understands.

"You could slouch," Kayla suggested.

"That is not a talent," I said.

Kayla shook her head. "That is a real shame, because you are a superb sloucher."

"I know," I sighed.

We sat and thought. I looked around the playground for ideas. I saw Lynette swinging on the swing set.

My stomach got tight and fluttery. *Why can't I be talented like Lynette? I bet she can even chew bubble gum better than me.*

I felt sorry for myself. Mom calls that having a pity party. Only too bad for me, because there was not even any cake.

"Well, I can't think of anything," Kayla finally said. She tied one end of her jump rope to a pole. "Plus I need someone to twirl the rope for me. Can you do it?"

"OK," I said.

It is hard to say no to a friend who needs help. That's why I cut Ryan's hair, even though it didn't turn out so well.

The whole time I twirled the rope, I thought about the talent show.

Then an idea popped *BLAM* into my head.

"I've got it!" I hollered, letting go of the rope. My end went flying through the air like a crazed snake. Kayla squealed and ducked.

"You got what?" Kayla untangled herself from the rope.

I smiled. "Yesterday Ryan and I read a whole stack of comic books. And oh boy, I laughed until my cheeks hurt." I laughed just to show her how funny it was.

Kayla stared at me. "And?"

"I can tell funny jokes, like in the comic

books! Everyone likes jokes."

That idea made Kayla clap. "My dad sometimes watches people tell jokes on television. He calls them chameleons."

"You mean comedians," I corrected. "A chameleon is a reptile lizard. Its skin changes color so it can hide in trees and grass and stuff. A comedian only hides in trees if his jokes aren't very funny."

"You're funny," Kayla said. "Tell me a joke."

"How about a knock-knock joke?"

"I like knock-knock jokes," Kayla said.

"OK," I said, rubbing my hands together. "Say 'knock-knock.'"

"Knock-knock," Kayla said.

"Who's there?" I asked.

Kayla frowned. "I don't know. This is *your* joke."

"Oops," I said. "Apparently there is a fine art to telling jokes."

"Try again," Kayla said.

I took a big breath. "Knock-knock."

"Who's there?"

"Ida."

"Ida who?"

"Ida wanna answer the door!"

Kayla laughed and laughed. It made me feel tickly inside. Then she said, "Tell me another one."

Suddenly I felt like a balloon without air. "You mean I have to tell more than one joke?"

"You can't have an act with only one joke."

I sighed. "You are right. Say 'knock-knock.'"

"Knock-knock," Kayla said.

"Who's there?" I asked.

Kayla groaned. "You did it again."

"Telling jokes is not as easy as it sounds."

"Timing is everything," Kayla agreed. "If you practice, I am sure you will get better."

"No, I won't," I said. "Apparently, to tell a knock-knock joke, you have to have a real knack-knack."

"And you lack the knack?"

I shook my head. "I don't even have a knick-knack paddywhack."

Kayla slouched. "Give the chameleon a bone."

Eye Buds

Clank, clank, clank, I tapped my spoon on the side of my glass.

Mom took a bite of meat loaf. "Meghan, why aren't you eating your dinner?"

I didn't look up. "I need talent."

"You need talent to eat?"

With a huffy breath, I crossed my arms. "No, I need talent for the talent show. Lynette plays the piano. Ryan dribbles. I can't do anything."

Setting her fork down, Mom sighed. "Meghan, did a flyer about a school talent show come home that I somehow missed?"

I bit my lip and nodded.

She held out her hand. "Will you get it for me, please?"

So I fetched that form. Uncrumpled it. Handed it over.

Mom slipped an arm around me and pulled me close. Smoothing out the edges of the paper, she began to read it. When she finished, I sniffled.

"Can you teach me how to play piano in three days?" I whispered. "Like Lynette?"

"Meghan, God gives each of us different talents. Don't compare yourself too much to other people. Just focus on what you can do best."

"I can't do anything best. But Lynette—"

Mom shushed me. "I don't want to hear about what Lynette can do. The Bible tells us to be content in all situations. Content with much . . . or with little." Then she patted my hand. "Besides, you have a lot to offer."

Now, I sat down and thought about what she said for a while. It seemed to me that might be a nice way of saying she can't teach me how to play the piano in three days.

Dad said, "Perhaps you could sing."

"Humph," I said. "I already tried that and it didn't work."

"You'll think of something."

That's when frustration came flying out of me.

"NO, I WON'T! Because thinking of something takes talent. AND SOMEHOW WE ARE ALL LACKING TALENT HERE!"

Then Dad told me to calm down and eat my dinner.

"Too bad EATING isn't a TALENT!" I shouted.

Mom and Dad got quiet then. I swallowed. And slouched. "Sorry. I was on a roll."

"Do you want to pray about it?" Mom suggested.

I perked up. Why hadn't I thought of

that? I like prayer. You talk to God, and he never looks at his watch.

I closed my eyes tight. "Dear God, sorry about that yelling thing. Please help me figure out what I do best. Otherwise I will look silly up on stage. And I don't want everyone to laugh at me. Amen."

I felt better after that, but my heart did a little tug. I knew I wasn't done. "And PS, God. I'm trying not to be jealous of Lynette, but I could use a little help there too."

Later, when Mom started cleaning up in the kitchen, I was still thinking and pushing mashed potatoes around on my plate. My potato pile looked just like a volcano.

And then, *BLAM!* Another idea popped into my head.

Once I had read in a science book about making a volcano by using kitchen ingredients. "Mom!" I yelled from the table. "May I have baking soda and vinegar to make a volcano?"

Mom splashed the dishes around in the sink. "Maybe after I'm done cleaning up."

Couldn't she hear the emergency in my voice?

I frowned. And waited. I waited for exactly one minute and fourteen seconds. But waiting is another talent I am apparently lacking.

So I sneakily crept out of my chair. To the kitchen door. Behind Mom. And right up to the cupboard.

Without even turning around, Mom said, "Get out of the cupboard."

I gasped. "How did you see me?"

She turned and winked at me. "I have eyes in the back of my head."

Extra eyes? How handy. It didn't look like she had extra eyes. Maybe her hair covered them up.

I tapped my chin. "Do I have eyes in the back of my head?"

Mom laughed. "Oh, no. You won't sprout extra eyes until you become a mommy. Then you'll know just what I'm talking about."

Very slowly, I reached my hand out and felt the back of my head. And what do you know? Just behind my ears I felt little round bumps.

"Mom!" I yelled. "Mom! I don't have eyes, but I do have EYE BUDS! And I never even knew that before! Wait until I tell Mrs. Arnold."

Leaning over, I flopped my hair forward to show Mom.

Mom looked at me for a long time. Then

she dried her hands on a towel. And rubbed her forehead. And sat down. And sighed.

"Is your volcano for the talent show?" she asked.

"Yes."

Smiling, Mom tucked some of my loose hair behind my ear.

"What a clever idea."

"Hey!" I covered up the back of my head with my hands. "Watch my eye buds, would you?"

5

Force of Nature

The next day, I felt kangaroo bouncy. So Kayla and I jumped rope all recess. Red-hot pepper. One foot. Backwards. Crisscross. I even made up a new jumping chant.

"Meghan flame-o
Has a big brain-o,
She's going to make a
Big volcano—
Spitting out lava,

Sizzle, sizzle, POP!
How many sizzles
Till it STOPS? 1, 2, 3, 4 . . ."

I made it all the way up to seventy-three sizzles before I missed. I couldn't wait to surprise everyone at the talent show with a real scientific model of a volcano. It felt like even I might explode.

After recess, Lynette leaned her chair back. She had a sour face. "What are you so excited about, Meghan?"

I grinned. "I've got so much talent, it will blow you away!"

Her eyes went wide. "What are you going to do?"

"I will unleash a powerful force of nature."

Her lip made a little pout. "I thought

Ryan was doing all the burping."

I shook my head at her. "Very funny. I'm talking about mixing together some ordinary kitchen supplies with explosive results."

Lynette gasped. "That sounds really dangerous."

"I know," I smirked, even though it wasn't dangerous at all. The vinegar and baking soda just foamed up like when you pour out soda pop.

Mom says I'm exaggerating when I make things seem bigger than they actually are. Which is a bad thing. Except when writers exaggerate in stories, they are using their imaginations. Which is a good thing.

So I told myself I was pulling my best writer imitation.

Mrs. Arnold cleared her throat. "Ladies, stop talking please."

Lynette waved her hand in the air. "But Mrs. Arnold! Meghan is scaring me!"

"I am not!"

"You are too!"

Then that girl gave Mrs. Arnold a trembling look like a scared rabbit. I am not exaggerating. "She's going to unleash a powerful force of nature at the talent show."

Mrs. Arnold raised one of her eyebrows.

By the way, have you ever tried doing that before? I have, but usually both of my eyebrows go up and down together like two copycat caterpillars. I can do it if I use my fingers. But that is cheating, I think.

Anyway, Mrs. Arnold can do it really well. "Meghan, what is she talking about?"

I didn't want to spoil the surprise of my act. "I can't tell you out loud. But I'll think about it, and you can look in my ear and check it out."

Mrs. Arnold sighed. "It doesn't work that way, dear. Let's go into the hall for a second."

Everyone was watching me. So I got up. And ducked my head. And walked slowly to the hall.

Mrs. Arnold closed the door behind us. "Well?" she asked.

I looked at the floor. "I made a volcano out of clay. I am going to fill it with baking soda. Then I am going to add some vinegar. It will look like lava is bubbling out of the volcano."

Mrs. Arnold nodded. "That's a clever idea. So why is Lynette upset?"

"She thinks I'm doing something dangerous. But I never actually said it was dangerous. Lynette is the one who said it sounded dangerous."

"But you let her think that it *was* dangerous."

I suddenly felt very small. And ashamed.

"I cannot play the piano," I whispered, almost to myself. "I am OK with that, really. Instead God gave me the talent to mix things up and cause reactions."

Mrs. Arnold laughed. "Yes, you can mix things up and cause reactions, Meghan Rose. You do a very good job at that."

I grinned a little.

Mrs. Arnold grinned back. "I think a volcano is a fine idea for the talent show. It's unusual and could add variety to the program. But try not to frighten your classmates, OK? I'll reassure Lynette that you won't try anything dangerous."

"OK," I said. "Mrs. Arnold, do you want to feel the eye buds on the back of my head? They are so cool."

Mrs. Arnold just gave me a look. I took a big breath so I could tell her even more about my eye buds, but she held up one finger and shook her head. Then she opened the door and marched me back to my seat.

What do you know? That one-finger trick worked on me too.

Mixing It Up

Finally the talent show tryout day for first grade arrived. After school I would make a model volcano while dressed up in my mad scientist white lab coat. Actually, it's a blue, polka-dotted bathrobe, but I'm pretending it's a white lab coat.

I wanted a mad scientist hairdo too. I used a lot of my dad's hair gel to make my hair stick out at wild angles.

I filled an empty water bottle with

vinegar and put it in the side pocket of my backpack. That way, if it spilled it wouldn't wreck everything inside my backpack.

I also carried a shoe-box top with the clay volcano right in the middle. The baking soda was already inside it.

As soon as I walked into the classroom, I grabbed Ryan. "See this, Ryan? This is my volcano. Don't you love it? I made it myself."

"That is fine work," he said.

I held up my signed permission form. "And see right here, Ryan? It says, 'Meghan Rose Thompson has my permission to perform THE AWESOME, AMAZING, INCREDIBLE, FRIGHTENING VOLCANO DEMONSTRATION. Signed, Mrs. Thompson. And PS. It is really hot.' I put that part in."

Lynette hung up her jacket. Sniffing, she pushed past me. Right then, part of me wished she'd mess up at the tryouts. I quickly told that part to be quiet. "What are you doing, Ryan?"

He grinned. "I'm dribbling and blowing bubbles, of course. I've been working on dribbling two balls at the same time."

"Wow," I said, very impressed.

Mrs. Arnold tapped my shoulder. "Lynette said you had a big 'globby' thing over here?"

I showed her my volcano. Mrs. Arnold took it. "Why don't we leave this on my desk until after school so it won't spill?"

The school day crawled by. I wiggled in my seat. I chewed my pencil. I was extra kangaroo bouncy at recess. But that was probably from my lack of waiting talent.

Even so, everything went fine until the end of the day.

You see, everyone has a classroom job. Sometimes you get to be paper passer-outer, or line leader, or lunch-box monitor.

Well, today Ryan's job was watering the plants. Only Ryan couldn't find the watering can. And he was in a hurry to get to the gym for the talent show tryouts. So guess what he did?

That boy took the water bottle right out of the side of my backpack and watered the plants.

At first I didn't notice the bottle was missing. I checked on my volcano. I stuffed my jacket and jump rope into the back of my backpack.

Then I felt the side pocket for my vinegar. And, oh boy, did panic hit.

"WHERE'S MY BOTTLE? WHERE'S MY BOTTLE?"

"Here," Ryan said, handing me back an empty water bottle.

"EEEEEEEEEEEEKKKKKKKKK!" I screeched. "EEK! EEK! EEK! EEK! WHAT HAPPENED TO MY VINEGAR?"

"Vinegar?" Ryan said. "I thought that was water. I watered the plants with it."

"NO! IT WAS VINEGAR FOR MY AWESOME, AMAZING, INCREDIBLE, FRIGHTENING VOLCANO DEMON-STRATION! WHICH I CANNOT DO WITHOUT VINEGAR!"

"Oh," he said. "I thought it smelled a little funny."

"A *little* funny?"

Ryan looked like he was shrinking. "I'm sorry, Meghan. I didn't mean to mess up

your talent show act."

I shook my permission slip at him. "I'M RUINED!" Snatching an eraser out of my desk, I rubbed out my whole form except for Mom's signature.

"If you want, you can chew gum for my act," Ryan offered.

I breathed nice and even. And patted Ryan on the shoulder. "You are very generous. But I don't want to wreck your act."

Ryan looked relieved. "OK. Then what are you going to do?"

I gulped. And tapped my lip. "I definitely need to pray again."

"I'll meet you in the gym," Ryan said. With a wave, he dashed out the door.

I plopped down at my desk. "Dear God," I said, "this is not going too well. I'm out of vinegar. And ideas. I need help again. And fast! Thanks for listening to me. I'll try to listen a little better to you too. Amen."

Even though I still didn't know what I'd do, I trusted God.

I looked at my blank form. I took out my purple marker. And in big letters I wrote TBA. To Be Announced.

And I hoped that by the time my turn rolled around, I would have something to announce.

Tryouts

When I got to the gym, Mrs. Arnold was collecting permission forms. Swinging my backpack out of the way, I handed her my paper.

Mrs. Arnold glanced at it as I walked by. Then she reached out and stopped me.

"TBA?"

I stood up straight. "To Be Announced. I think. I hope."

Mrs. Arnold frowned. "Meghan, where

is the clay volcano you stored on my desk all day?"

I twisted the bottom of my shirt. "It's still there. But change of plans, Mrs. Arnold. Unless you have some extra vinegar I can borrow."

"No, I don't. And what happened to your vinegar?"

"Your plants drank it."

Mrs. Arnold looked up to the ceiling. And counted to five real quiet. And sighed.

"Do you have any idea what you're doing? Because I don't want you to get embarrassed if you stand in front of everybody and then draw a blank."

"Don't worry," I said. "I'm a pretty good drawer. So I bet if I had paper and pencil I could draw a really good blank."

Mrs. Arnold said, "Fine. Sit down."

I felt her watch me walk all the way to the bleachers.

I sat next to Ryan. He was blowing bubbles. "Hey, Meghan. How did your praying go?"

"Really well," I said.

"What are you going to do?"

I shrugged. "I have noooo idea."

Mrs. Arnold quieted everyone down. "Do I have everyone's permission forms?"

We all nodded our heads.

"Good. Please be a polite audience while waiting for your turn. No talking or running around when someone is performing. When the performer finishes, you may clap. No negative comments."

Mrs. Arnold gave us one of her looks. We all sat very still. Or tried to, anyway.

"Each performer or group of performers

must announce their names and what they are going to do before they start. Please speak slowly and clearly into the microphone. If you have a recording of music to accompany your act, give it to me first. Any questions?"

We all shook our heads.

"Your parents will pick you up at four o'clock. Tomorrow you will receive a note stating whether or not your act was chosen for the school talent show. Now, who's ready to start tryouts?"

We all cheered. Except me.

I was looking around at glittery leotards, fancy dresses, and tip-tap shoes. With one hand, I reached up and touched my crazy, mad scientist hair. Suddenly my tummy felt a little sickish.

Mrs. Arnold ruffled her stack of papers.

"First up, Ryan Baker."

Holding a basketball under each arm, Ryan stepped up to the microphone. "Hi. My name is Ryan, and I'm going to dribble two basketballs and blow bubbles at the same time."

With a big grin, Ryan started dribbling one ball, then two, right in rhythm. When he started blowing a bubble, he fumbled a little bit with the balls until one was up when the other was down.

The bubble got bigger and bigger and bigger. The balls got more and more wild.

Then *POP!* Gum stretched right over his nose. And stuck.

At that point, Ryan lost control. One of the balls hit the edge of the piano and shot off toward me. Ryan dribbled the other ball off his foot, and it went flying at Mrs. Arnold.

"Aaaahhh!" Mrs. Arnold yelled, ducking out of the way. The ball crashed into a stack of folding chairs. They toppled with a loud *CRASH! WHAM! BOOM!*

After all that noise, it seemed very quiet when Mrs. Arnold straightened herself back up in her seat.

Ryan pulled the gum off his face. "Ta da?" he said, real soft.

"Very. Nice." Mrs. Arnold said, as she picked up forms that had flown to the ground. "You may sit down now."

Ryan plopped down next to me. His face looked hot and embarrassed, plus he still had tiny pieces of green gum sticking to his mouth. Poor guy.

Forgetting all about my sickish tummy, I patted his leg. "You are so brave going first, Ryan. And dribbling two basketballs is amazing, even if one hit your foot."

"Really?" he whispered.

I smiled at him. "Really."

He looked much relieved after that.

"Lynette   Becker,"   Mrs.   Arnold
announced. "You're next."

Lynette stood and smoothed her dress out.
Her legs seemed wobbly as she walked up
to the microphone. She opened her mouth to
tell everyone her name — then her eyes went
wide. She snapped her mouth shut again.

"Lynette?" Mrs. Arnold prompted.

On Stage, Everybody!

Lynette licked her lips.

"MynameisLynetteBeckerandI'm goingtoplayYankeeDoodleDandyonthe piano."

She stumbled to the piano bench and sat down.

PLINK, PLINK, PLINK, she played. Then stopped. Shook her head. Started over.

PLINK, PLINK, PLINK.

Then she stopped again. And shook her

head harder. And started over.

PLINK, PLINK, PLINK.

I leaned over to Ryan and whispered, "Didn't we just hear those notes?"

"Shhh," he said. "I like this song. That girl has talent."

Meanwhile Lynette had stopped again.

Then what do you know? She stood up. And started crying. And ran out of the gym.

Kids around me started whispering and laughing to each other. I felt sorry for wishing Lynette would mess up. And now that she had messed up, I felt even worse.

I tell you, the good feeling of cheering for someone sure beats the bad feeling of rooting against them.

"Boy, I'm glad you didn't make fun of me, Meghan," Ryan said.

That's when it hit me. I knew what my talent was! I'd had it all along.

Mrs. Arnold clapped her hands to get our attention. She had a funny look on her face—like she smelled something bad but was pretending she didn't. "Well," she said. "I can't wait to see who's up next."

I waved my hand in the air. "Mrs. Arnold. Shouldn't someone check on Lynette?"

She gave me a weak smile. "Are you volunteering?"

"Yes," I said. "I'll be back soon." I scooped up my backpack and ran out after Lynette.

I found Lynette sitting on the restroom floor. Her eyes looked puffy. She sniffled at me. "What do *you* want?"

I put my hands on my hips. "Ryan ruined my act. He used my vinegar to water the classroom plants. So I am looking for a piano player to join my new act."

"But I c-c-couldn't play at all," Lynette hiccuped.

"That's because you were by yourself and everyone was watching you."

"My tummy flip-flopped. My hands got shaky. And I forgot all the notes."

I shrugged. "It could have gone better. I bet if everyone looked at me instead of you, you could play."

Lynette bit her lip. Rubbing her eyes, she sat up straight. "Maybe. But what will you do? You're not going to release a powerful force of nature, are you?"

"Not unless you have some vinegar." I gave her my best sneaky schemer look and reached into my backpack.

I pulled out my jump rope. "I have a

better idea. Right now I am feeling kangaroo bouncy. Whatever you play, I can jump to the beat. Then all the pressure is off you."

Slowly, Lynette stood. "It just might work."

I held out my hand. "Partners?"

She shook it. "Partners. But if we get picked for the show, you've got to change your hair."

I'd forgotten about my gelled-up hair. "Don't you like my mad scientist style?"

Lynette frowned.

Then I started laughing. And she started laughing. And we laughed all the way back to the gym.

We arrived just in time to see Mallory Smith wearing a tall, striped hat and screeching out the last notes of "Happy Birthday, Dr. Seuss."

We were back in our bleacher seats by the time Mallory finished bowing. I actually think Mrs. Arnold's face lit up when she saw me.

"Next performer, Meghan Thompson."

I looked at Lynette. She took a big breath and nodded. We linked arms and stepped up to the microphone.

I spoke loud and clear. "Actually, I am no longer a solo act. I have a new partner. And so you can erase that TBA on my sheet, Mrs. Arnold. Because I am OSN . . . On Stage Now. I am Meghan Rose Thompson!"

"And I am Lynette Becker," Lynette said.

"Lynette will play 'Yankee Doodle' on the piano."

"And Meghan will unleash a powerful force of jump-roping nature."

When Lynette started playing, I started jumping.

PLINK. *PLINK*. JUMP. JUMP.

I even made up a new jump chant right on the spot. And good news! Mrs. Arnold didn't make any faces while we performed.

"Yankee Doodle
Went to town,
A-riding on a cow-ow.
Then he stopped to
Make a friend
And so he's happy now-ow!
Yankee Doodle,
Keep it up,
Yankee Doodle Dandy.
Find the music, play it loud,
And with the rope be handy!"

The way Lynette's face seemed to glow when we finished made me feel bouncy on the inside.

Everyone clapped and clapped. We held hands and bowed.

Lynette and I were both right about something. She is the best piano player in first grade. And among other things, I am good at mixing things up and causing a reaction.

Real Talent

The next day, Lynette jumped rope with Kayla and me at recess.

"Do you think Mrs. Arnold chose Ryan's act?" Kayla asked.

Lynette shrugged. "I hope so. He was hilarious."

"Yeah," I said, "only he wasn't supposed to be funny. So that's a problem."

"I don't think Mallory made it," Lynette said.

Kayla crossed her arms. "She's going to be sad. Her mom bought that costume special."

When the recess bell rang, Kayla scooped up the rope. "I wish I could have jumped with you, Meghan. I could have jumped backwards."

"Now that would have been a nice addition," I said as we ran to line up.

Just when it seemed the end of school and the delivery of talent show invitations might never come, Mrs. Arnold handed me a card.

It read, "Congratulations! Your act called On Stage Now has been selected for the All School Talent Show. Please practice your act at home. Ask a parent for help. Rehearsals will be in the gym at 3:00 next Wednesday and Thursday. The talent show starts at 1:00

on Friday. Parents welcome!"

My eyes got big while I read. "LYNETTE! WE MADE IT!" I shouted.

I felt volcano bubbly. Kangaroo bouncy. Yip-yippee happy.

Lynette turned around. We jumped up and down and hugged each other.

I felt so happy and proud, I almost missed the look on Ryan's face. It wasn't a happy look. It was a my-fish-just-died look.

Then I realized. He didn't get invited. Some of my excitement got squeezed out of me like water squeezed from a sponge.

"I'm sorry, Ryan," I said, patting his back.

Ryan turned away. I gulped and asked, "Who else from our class made it?"

"No one. Mallory sang. Kind of. Adam tried some yo-yo tricks, but his yo-yo didn't go up and down. It just went down. Then he whirled the string around and accidentally knocked over a CD player. Abigail twirled a hula hoop on her arm, but it flew off and hit Mrs. Arnold on the head."

Frowning, I looked around the room. All those kids seemed disappointed. Very disappointed.

A hand touched my shoulder. Mrs. Arnold smiled down at Lynette and me. "Congratulations, ladies. I only picked three first grade acts—one from our class and two from Mrs. Taylor's room. You did a nice job. You should feel proud."

I looked down. "Yeah, only I don't feel so good, Mrs. Arnold."

Mrs. Arnold pursed her lips. "You're a talented jumper, and Lynette played well. Together you made a great team."

A lump formed in my throat, like I'd swallowed peanut butter. "Jumping? But that isn't my talent, Mrs. Arnold."

She looked confused. "Then what is?"

"Mrs. Arnold," I said, ignoring her question. "Can Lynette and I add a few people to our act?"

I looked at Lynette. She gave me a small smile and nodded.

"It wouldn't really change it that much," I said. "It's just that if I can jump rope to music, maybe Kayla can join our act and jump too. Then what about letting Ryan dribble just one basketball with us? Maybe Mallory can put on her costume and introduce us. And Adam can stand in one place and yo, since apparently he can't yo-yo. Abigail can help me chant. And we can all do it while Lynette plays."

I could see Ryan out of the corner of my eye. He gave me the thumbs-up and crossed his fingers. Kayla, Mallory, Adam, and Abigail stood near him, whispering to each other and watching with big eyes.

Mrs. Arnold rubbed her forehead. "Well. Interesting idea. But I don't think so. It would be best if you just kept it at two. Less chance for something to go wrong."

My tummy fluttered. "But I prayed for an idea, Mrs. Arnold," I whispered. "And I thought about what I do best. And it isn't jumping. Or chanting. Or even causing reactions. It's being a friend. That's my talent. Being a friend. And if this is really a talent show, friendship ought to be a talent that takes center stage, I think."

Mrs. Arnold stood, real quiet, for a long time. Then she smiled. "OK, you win,

Meghan. You can add a few friends to the act."

I heard Ryan whoop and Mallory squeal. They ran over to us, and we threw our arms around each other and jumped up and down.

"We're in the show! We're in the show! We're in the show!" we chanted, real happy.

Mrs. Arnold shooed us out of the room. "Get going already. School's over! I expect you to practice hard this weekend."

"We will," I promised.

Mrs. Arnold ran her fingers through her hair. "Good. I'll be keeping my eyes on you."

I grinned. "Even the ones in the back of your head?"

Lessons

Teachers always know whether or not you do your homework. You could give them any kind of logical excuse when it's missing, but they always seem to know when you are exaggerating.

For example, Mrs. Arnold did not believe me when I told her an octopus reached out of my toilet and dragged my math worksheet down the pipes.

It was only a small exaggeration. My

homework did go down the pipes when I accidentally tore it into tiny pieces and flushed it. But my point is, there may have been an octopus waiting down there, for all she knows.

Anyway, promising Mrs. Arnold we would practice seemed the same as promising to do our homework. For sure she would know if we didn't keep our word.

We were happy to do this homework though. We practiced all weekend.

Even so, hurray for rehearsal. Adam learned he could not swing his yo-yo so close to the microphone. Kayla learned to stop jumping when the music ended, even if she was on a roll. And Ryan learned it wasn't a good idea to use a small bouncy ball instead of a basketball. You just can't control those tiny all-over-the-place things.

We did more than just practice. We coordinated our wardrobes. Mom bought us white T-shirts—the cheapy ones you find in the craft store. Then we painted our handprints on them and wrote ON STAGE in glitter glue.

Mallory's mom bought everyone tall striped hats. I tell you, that was a stroke of smarts. We looked like a regular, hand-picked, Cat-in-the-Hat army!

No question about it. We were a team.

Too bad Mrs. Arnold made us take off the hats while we waited for our turn to perform. Apparently she feared those tall striped things were too distracting.

All that practice paid off. We were a hit!

Mallory did a great-skate-fate-plate-crate-date Dr. Seuss-style introduction. Ryan did not dribble the ball off his foot. Kayla and I jumped up a storm. Abigail chanted loud and clear. Adam did a yo. But it was an interesting yo because he fell down when he did it.

And Lynette really was a star. Without her zippy tune, nothing else would have gone so well.

When we finished, we all held hands and bowed. Everyone clapped and clapped.

It felt good performing on stage. Not because everyone cheered for us, but because I did it with my friends.

When we took our seats, Lynette sat next to me.

"Meghan," she whispered, "thank you. I don't think I could have done it without you."

I squeezed her hand. "No, thank you. Because of you, I figured out my talent. And I have a lot to offer. By the way, do you want to feel my eye buds?"

Together we felt the bumps on the back of my head. I can't wait until they grow.

You know, happy feels better than jealous. For one thing, you smile when you are happy. And smiling doesn't hurt your face as much as frowning, unless your lips are chapped.

For another, feeling jealous turns your insides into knots instead of giggles. And that's *knot* fun.

So I am happy.

Happy I helped Lynette get over her stage fright and play that funky music. Happy my best friends joined in on the fun. Happy God lets me talk to him with prayer when I don't know what to do. Happy God made me kangaroo bouncy.

Most of all, I'm glad I have a new friend. Yes, sir. And although she's not kangaroo bouncy, she sure is yankee doodle dandy!

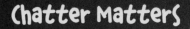
Chatter Matters

1. Who is your best friend? What do you like most about him or her? What do you do best as a friend?

2. What is something you do really well? How can you use that talent to bring glory to God? What do you wish you could do better? What can you do to get better at it?

3. How does prayer help you deal with difficult emotions or tough situations? Can you think of a time when God answered your prayer?

4. How is exaggeration like lying? How is it different?

5. What does the Bible say about jealousy? With your mom or dad's help, read these passages from the Bible: Proverbs 14:30; Proverbs 27:4; James 3:16; 1 Peter 2:1.

Blam! – Great Activity Ideas

1. Make a volcano. Using regular modeling clay, form a conical volcano shape with a hole big enough to hold ½ cup of baking soda. If you don't have clay to make a volcano shape, just use a cup.

Put ¼ to ½ cup of baking soda at the bottom of the "volcano." Mix a few drops of red food coloring with 1 cup of vinegar. Pour the vinegar mixture over the baking soda and watch it bubble up!

What's really happening? The baking soda reacts with the acid in the vinegar to produce a gas called carbon dioxide. It's the forming of this gas that makes the bubbles!

2. Bubble gum! Buy a pack of bubble gum (or ask your parents to buy you one) and share it with a friend.

3. Joke book. Check out a joke book from your local library. Read it with a friend.

4. Make a friendship T-shirt. You can do this alone (with your parent's help) or with friends. Get a plain, white, cotton T-shirt. Lay down paper or an old cloth to protect your table or floor. Then paint your hand with acrylic paint. Stretch out your fingers and press your hand on the T-shirt, keeping your hand and fingers flat.

Repeat the paint-and-press step. Try using

a variety of paint colors. With a permanent marker, write your name under one of your handprints.

5. Showtime. Put on a show for your family or friends. Sing, dance, read a story, model clothes, dribble a basketball—whatever you want. Just have fun! If you include a friend in your plans, he or she can be a part of the action.

For Jim, Michael, and Meghan—LZS

For Sarah—SC

Lori Z. Scott graduated from Wheaton College
eons ago. She is a second-grade teacher, a wife, the
mother of two busy teenagers, and a writer. Lori has
published over one hundred articles, short stories,
devotions, puzzles, and poems and has contributed
to over a dozen books.

In her spare time Lori loves doodling, reading the
Sunday comics, and making up lame jokes.

You can find out more about Lori and her books
at www.MeghanRoseSeries.com.

Stacy Curtis is a cartoonist, illustrator,
printmaker, and twin who's illustrated over twenty
children's books, including a *New York Times* best
seller. He and his wife, Jann, live in Oak Lawn,
Illinois, and happily share their home with their dog,
Derby.

Meghan Rose
is bouncing
your way!

978-0-7847-2103-2

978-0-7847-2105-6

978-0-7847-2106-3

978-0-7847-2107-0

978-0-7847-2930-4

978-0-7847-2931-1

978-0-7847-2932-8

978-0-7847-2933-5

**To order these titles
visit www.standardpub.com
or call 1-800-543-1353.**